Embracing the Razor

By the same author:

The Art Of The Monologue, 2008
Shakespeare's World (with David Allen) 2006
The Warhorse, 1987
Machiavelli, Machiavelli, 1986

Embracing the Razor

John Upton

PUNCHER & WATTMANN

First published in 2014

Published by Puncher & Wattmann
PO Box 441
Glebe NSW 2037

http://www.puncherandwattmann.com

puncherandwattmann@bigpond.com

National Library of Australia
Cataloguing in Publication entry:

Upton, John
Embracing the Razor

ISBN   9781922186621

I. Title

A821.3

Cover design by Matthew Holt

Printed by McPhersons Printing Group

This project has been assisted by the
Australian Government through the
Australia Council, its arts funding and
advisory body.

Australian Government

Australia Council for the Arts

Contents

Grief

Embracing the Razor

Destinations

Rhymes and Rhizomes

Grief

Ashley Who Is Catherine

"I'm trying to save you, stupid!" Darting dustpan and broom,
tiny lizard in the bedroom, god knows how, the cat —
lizard flees beneath the bed, but Ashley
shuts the door (the cat), rolls castors, flicks
the terrified black scrap into her fisted
plastic maw, then scrambles through the house
to the back garden. Rescue is a mission.

Patron saint of waifs and strays, herself adopted
at three, she'd lead stray animals home from school.
Her birth certificate said Catherine, but
her mother, alcoholic and five other kids
to a here-and-gone housebreaker husband
now called her Ashley — so her adopting family
took up the name that the child responded to.

But Catherine now had a bureaucratic
name-force. From birth certificate, it elbowed into
rent agreements, onto her driver's licence.
One life became two separate identities,
a loving present and a living past. When people
wondered, Ashley took them through it patiently,
sharp partisan for nurture over nature.

She ran a complaints department for a jewellery firm,
disentangling grievances from scams. The staff
marvelled at her temperament. She married
happily, adopting dogs and cats from shelters
as she never wanted children of her own.
Her last life was escape from psychic rubble,
but that first life pinned the child buried alive.

ICU

is a fortress, you press a button
and wait
like some malevolent bacterium.
"I'm here to see my wife"
a click, a heavy sliding. Arterial corridors
a nurse at a station
an orderly with a trolley of folded white sheets.
Another nurse, a tiny ante-room.

Hygiene is vital: over your clothes, you pull
a white gown of tough matt paper, you tie the back
slip on a face-mask, elastic behind your ears –
your breathing's toxic.
An electric ecology –
bed, ventilator, ECG, all centred
on your wife, invaded by pneumonia.
Somehow you've reached the soul.

You hold her hand, you smile
and watch those eyes
see past this, past today
backwards into both-of-you.

Nurses come and go, shifts start and end.
You sit, you walk, you stow the useless gown
and mask into a rubbish bin for burning.
The hospital exhales you.

Talk

A radio talks faintly in this huge
hospital carpark, a desert of panic nosed
into dutiful bays. I pause
in halogen-grubby dark — I can't see the source
but my ear plucks out the words "Beethoven's Ninth".
I wait. The music opens, swells, commands. Then
someone turns it off. A vast dark nothingness.
I head inside.

At the lift, two people. Polite smiles. "It takes a while",
he says. I offer. "Yes". In this desperate place
somehow we need to touch.
"It's on the seventh", she adds, feeling foolish.
They don't seem to be together.
We watch the numbered light ascending.
Like a saint, I think. I'm not religious.
"The other one's coming down", he mutters. Steel jaws
wide enough to gulp a bed and nurses
creep open horizontally. I press Intensive Care.
They don't say anything.

The ventilator mask on Ashley's face
divides us, and our impulses are opposite —
breathless, she wants to talk, I'm urging rest.
The doctors were abrupt, "It could be days,
it could be hours". This is Saturday,
on Friday she seemed scarcely ill — now the whole world
is cancer and pneumonia. Lungs deprived,
she won't stop speaking: "The cat shall need —
fresh mince. And finish my tax return —
it's on the desk".
Her tax return? "You have to rest".
Her sister must have her car,

her niece her amethyst ring.
"The car keys —
are on top of the glass-fronted —
cabinet that holds the ornaments".
It comes to me this list is not a list,
but outflung arms between us, holding on.

Morphine Around Midnight

We started her on morphine around midnight,
just enough to keep her comfortable,
the nurse says. The ECG machine
is beeping by the bed.
She probably can hear you.
I sit and whisper for a sign. Nothing. I talk
quietly about Lyon, on our circuit
of the capitals arriving mid-afternoon
at the railway station, aching to make love,
and doing so among our piled suitcases
in the garret of that ancient high hotel.
The memory now is packed in coded phrases
the nurse won't understand, but you will, in there
in your morphine overcoat. By now it's Sunday,
the doctors said that if you live till Monday
then you live. The nurse is quiet,
professional, busy with tubes and dials and pillows.
The room is in a stupor. The monitor
paces.

By noon, with family here, I need to make calls,
feed the cat. *You might be home by Friday.*
I move towards the ante-room. The nurse
touches my arm, says I should stay. I've barely
registered the surgeon in the doorway,
that small nod. Now she removes the ventilator
mask and tapes a tube into your nose,
a barest pinch of oxygen. Pneumonia
is at its work. My
mind is saying,
They need the beds. The
capitals of Europe are laid waste.
I ask the nurse,

"How long?" "Not long".
One hour, five minutes.

Silence

I close the door, it's there, the street's absence
corporeal, a rigid silence tangible
as laying on of hands. Before was friendly,
even when she was out the quiet was warm —
mammalian, occupied, comfortable. Now
the quiet is a stiffness, like a frost
that doesn't crackle underfoot. She carried
warm stillness of her own, like at a concert,
the moment after Beethoven before
the hands, the skin erect, the mind enthused,
a hush so taut it seems to vibrate. Vanished. Chilled.
Now there's drained absence, the room the universe.
Arriving, I've closed the door, the room is unaware.
The shopping makes a thump and plastic whisper
on the kitchen bench. Quiet flickers off and on
like a faulty neon. I walk into the bedroom,
change my clothes in denim's woven, casual
muttering as silence sucks its bones.
A thin bereftitude.
I chat with the electric jug
and it gives me a minute. I make coffee,
then I confront the morning newspaper,
dodging the politics, creeping instead among
the 'human interest", criminals and courts,
plumbing silence for its solitude.

Fire

The rocks and tiles of afternoon are radiant,
pumping sun back at sun. The bitumen
in the carpark bakes as motors switch off and die. Dark suits
hover, lock, then head for shade. Greetings
are murmured, handshakes, kisses, stoic – not
glad, out of respect. I press flesh,

> The bush is burning, half the State's on fire,
> you watch the orange torrent stride the valleys
> on TV, while I ignore it, trying
> to despatch yesterday's paper, they keep piling up.
> You hate the heat, complain, "It's going to be
> a long hot summer". I shrug indifferently:
> "It is what it is". Nothing from you except
> a quick, sharp look.

nod, am grateful.
Ten minutes late, the previous crowd debouches.
Inside, the chapel's cool. You're waiting, you who had
a dread of earth, who wanted this. I speak,
hold on. We play

Beside your bed, I'm looking at the heavy mask
that's strapping you to life. The nurse,
thinking to make you comfortable
turns a dial to Warm, but suddenly
you fight the heat, tearing at straps, webbing
to rip the mask off
and lie there dying in cool breathlessness
as the monitor riots and the rushing nurse
switches off Warm and straps your life back on
while I watch, stranded and remote.

your music, Pachelbel
and Beatles, ending with Here Comes the Sun. Then, clamped
inside the half-hour timetable, you wait alone
as one by one your mourners follow me
out of cool shade into the violent heat.

Clearing the Bathroom

The Herald's *Good Weekend* doesn't disappear
to the bathroom any more while I'm wrapped in the news.
I find a pile of them
mixed with her gardening magazines and glossies
on the floor beside the toilet. I gather them up.
I miss their weekly vanishing.

On a tiled ledge
in easy reach of the pedestal, her glasses
sit on a pile of books. In the ridiculous way
that life wrong-foots me, the book on top is called
They Went That-a-Way, an almanac
on the deaths of the famous, infamous and great.
Her glasses are stylish,
large, studious lenses, narrow metal frame,
brown trim to match her eyes. Her eye for detail
was acute; she'd painted once. Lately she'd say
I'm in the bathroom, turn on the extractor fan,
close the door, flip open cigarettes and,
that one finished, stub it in the ashtray
and light another. The lungs breathed out, the breath
was sucked away.

I take the *Good Weekends*
into the living room and put the ashtray,
empty now, into the bin. Her glasses
I leave in the bathroom, resting on her books.

Beverley

Eight elongated weeks since Ashley died, while I'm
still snarled and struggling in the web of it, her
missing voice, the emptiness of rooms, the
customary habits being torn up like
old floorboards, and unaccustomed ones laid down,
my intercom buzzes. It's Ellen. I don't know Ellen. No,
she's the best friend of Beverley next door. Can she
see me? Beverley died last night. Of cancer.

No, it wasn't sudden. I've been vacuuming,
the barrel's in the middle of the floor, the pipe
is propped against the couch. Ellen won't sit.
Beverley was diagnosed six months ago. Divorced,
living alone, she told only Ellen, while she had
all the procedures, chemo, radiology. Now
I'm remembering when her hair was different, lighter, cropped.
I almost asked if she was dating, thank God I didn't.

With Ashley it was different, undiagnosed, gone
within two days – for months my wife
was dying and I didn't know. And now, within
eight weeks, it's happened again. Ellen is saying,
"It's sad Bev wasn't speaking to her kids, they didn't
know she was in hospital, she didn't want
them there, it was just me". I nod, not asking why. And Ellen
leaves to clean next door, she'll call if I can help her.

A few days after Ashley died, I found a card
from Bev, hand written, in my letterbox. It read:
"Cherish your life together, and those memories
will bring you comfort". She must have carried grief
like a child for months, while giving me "Good morning"
as I passed. Inside these empty rooms, I vacuum,
stunned by ghosts and strangely twice-bereaved.

Daisy

Cat shit in the bath again – amazingly,
you can love a remnant, a totemic
ritual, a disagreeable thing
framed as a person, so you become that person's
duty. Ashley always cleaned the bath
for Daisy; in the netherness of loss,
the raw acuity, it's passed to me, although
I never liked cats much. Since Ashley died,
house and the day have new dynamics: Daisy
used to have litter, but preferred the bath,
so shit and disinfectant are my instruments
of reassurance that I'm needed
in these empty rooms.
Coping with the guts of daily living
has small compensations: Daisy's at the door
when I come home. She charges up the hall,
then stops at the bedroom doorway to be sure
I'm following. It seems she can forget
more easily than I can, or she understands
better about living in the moment,
seizing its brief ecstasy. She croons
as I stroke her. These, it seems, are remnants
towards something, and I gather them.

Paperwork

The application form to bury you
in the memorial garden beside your parents
is lost, the salesman on the phone is saying, the
office, they've looked everywhere, it's awful,
they're so sorry. The telephone receiver
in my hand has a zapping quality, a distancing
effect, that in the middle of my losing you
they've lost you. And there's guilt
at this end of the line, too, more than his,
that our connection, umbilical without
benefit of children, is disrespected.
This process is all mine, you hated earth,
the thought of waking there, you wanted fire,
the fiercer, quicker element, which I gave to you.
You came back home with me in bridal white,
white as polystyrene. For four months,
you waited on the lowboy, incompleteness,
with half my life, which was our life, thirty years,
made a different entity, burned away.
My first intention was our scrap of garden
along the fence, fringing the tiles. Impractical,
too narrow. Then the thought, your parents,
whom you loved, the memorial garden.
Now the salesman keeps insisting, *the site's*
still there, we've kept the place, it's just
the form, so regrettable, we're so sorry.
How to calm the office, repair their loss?
We settle on him faxing a blank form for me
to fill in – or is it out? – and return, a.s.a.p.

Ashes to Ashes

Two kookaburras shout their territory,
the salesman is delighted, says
it's a sign, so appropriate. I don't think it's a sign
except that this place is peaceful
and you'd like it. It's just me
and your sister. The wake was months ago.

You've lain in that polystyrene box at home,
clunky and square, while you and I discussed
your future. Confinement was the issue:
you'd only wear a bra when you were going out
and coffins appalled you, the thought of waking up, trapped.
But we both know polystyrene is a visitor,
transitional. I understand this garden
is a betrayal, but a small one, surely.

The gardener stands back,
hands crossed before his crotch, birth and death, I suppose —
the salesman hands me you
in the copper box to shield you from gravel, sand
and roots of trees that should join you
to those singing kookaburras, as you'd want.
But that's how they do things here. I'm startled that
in my arms you weigh so much, almost as much
as on our wedding day, across the threshold.
I put you into the ground, then scoop in earth
and bed it, bed it, round.

There's a separate box, a compartment
something like this cylinder,
inside me, where all this lives.

I step back. Julie scoops in sandy loam.
The kookaburras are going off again.
The gardener waits to finish as we step onto
the golf cart with the salesman, who's still marvelling
at nature and its bounty. Back at his desk
he writes the last receipt.

Embracing the Razor

The Marriage Counsellor's Diary

"I don't do this", she says, naked in bed
this conference weekend. "Neither do I".
Two marriage counsellors, startled as to why
at the first night Welcome party. Craziness,
simpatico, divorce. I've lost my head –
still in the lift we started to undress.

She says she'll call. I work but wait all day.
Marty and Mary feel they've lost the passion,
I have new thoughts; though it's a heavy session,
they're happier. I'm not. No telephone.
Then when it rings I don't know what to say.
I'm too screwed up from living on my own.

The movie, an old Ken Russell, is so bad
we laugh and groan. The restaurant is slack,
we wait for half an hour with friends, then sack
it for one of those sleazy little dives
with a broken neon up a lane, and have
one of the best evenings of our lives.

"The good things make love worth it", Cate's insisting.
"No, they don't", says Barry, "Because I'm dying".
"You're dead" she tells him, "Stop your bloody crying,
I'm here, aren't I?" I try a lighter tack,
but as I see them out, he's still persisting.
She telephones to say they won't be back.

Knowing the rules, the histories and the case
studies won't help. You know you're compromised,
and yet you're still as mortally surprised
as any other idiot. "It's gone",
she says, "It's over. Sorry. There's a place
for rent". The practice saves you, holding on.

Embracing the Razor

The man with the raised razor is our friend, my love.
His intention is intricate, he'll slice across
the meadow of my cornea, where light
showers in and weds you to my retina.

The anaesthetist was chattily familiar,
taking his time, like meeting me in a pub,
and then a simple cannula in my arm. He's good,
I'm relaxed with eye clawed open and surgeon poised.

Now the razor's cutting carefully across
the eye's soft tissue, with the pressured edges
rising as in *Un Chien Andalou*,
my flesh weeping with shock. He'll slip my vision out

and replace the living tissue with a piece
of manufactured plastic, with a use-by
ten years hence. And it shall sharpen you.
I'm told I love this science. I think I do.

Applause

Wired up, she walks on, she's eleven,
cameras roll, the T.V. judges smirk
in holy patience, and in the cavernous dark
the stoked but unlit fire of the audience.
Starting small, she sings, this child, of love
and lust and one night only; primal passion
stirs in the body of the audience,
tight shots of faces glowing, then over-sized

and well rehearsed spontaneous applause,
close-ups of piscine gawping from the judges.
A misdirected longing stirs the stadium,
not for the child but for a collective beast,
a staged abandoning of inhibition,
approved hysteria, an existential
turning from its tawdry insensate opposite
sprawled in a nation's dying living rooms.

In the gladiatorial raping of an angel
a people reaches for a paper cup
of meaning, for a gulp of altar wine.
One night, a child, fast-cuts, a line of judges –
the audience applauds a savage construct
in the universe's face with the intensity
of North Korean generals as they scream and clap
the Dear Leader, applauding for their lives.

It's over. An atmospheric lying back.
The child is shy and humble. The four judges
are theatrical and overwhelmed,
it's, "O - M - G". "Amazing". Four thumbs-up.
T.V. has done its work, the undertow
is running and the rough dreaming of millions
holds shape, while in the provinces of feeling
North Korea prepares to go to war.

Day Surgery

Face in morning mirror is
a scrunched cloth mat
in hard light, uncomposed sonata
falling into form.

Railway station
the Salvation Army major renting smiles
outside, hope is a gold mine. I don't go there.

Sonata's found its instruments, yelling traffic,
trains brawling. Faces
out to lunch, closed for repairs, available
for rent, cheap

Receptionists fed twice daily with politeness
racks of chairs screwed
to carpet, voices hushed as
credit cards change hands
sliding steel cabinets of secrets.
My mother was here once.

She died at fiftytwo. Breast cancer. She
delivered eight children, never complained. Though
after the diagnosis, said an aunt once,
she thumped her palm against a cupboard door:
"Why? Why?!"

Surgeon's chat is sports and weather –
we're alone.
Words are tongs to hold facts
at a distance.
Freckle on right calf: needle
in surgeon's plastic hand, pain the

wrong way round, rampaging local
(aaahh! / are you okay? / that hurts / yes it does a bit / aaarghh!)
scalpel no pain at all
extracting the vivid mushroom
sleeping fatal baby.

Is this what it's about?

e$=$mc^2

They got it right, the old Bulletin cartoonists,
the toothbrush moustache with the mechanical
right arm raised, and the deformed leg dashing about
behind him. They captured perfectly the Emperor's
thick glasses in the rising sun; they caught
the folksy president in the open car
driving to blast some dam or other. And now and then
they sketched that unkempt hairline's sunburst silhouette,
the Nobel winner stranded in Belgian sand-dunes
as his books burned in Berlin.

But they all missed it, and how could they not
in the tumult of Jack Lang's
coathanger moustache, in the ploughman's
struggle with Depression prices –
that tiny event, the blown seed in the chaotic furrow
missed also in Berlin, in Tokyo, in Washington
as the most famous hairline in the world
took its bomb-blast outline from the beach,
strode aboard the liner in Southampton
leaving behind a lifetime's pacifism
sailing towards Manhattan.

Scissors

Watching her, it frightens me. As scissors
trim yellow paper on the kitchen bench
to wrap two books she's bought her niece, the wall
above our stove's a Post-It gallery
of stickers nominating dates for birthdays,
doctor's appointments, cinema with friends,
the day the cat can have fresh meat again
(one day in three), set in her lovely cursive.
Everything's normal, organised, it says
but contradicts itself. She asks for sticky tape
I've given her already. I indicate
she nods and smiles, "I'm tired, that's all". She puts
books on the sheet to check the paper size.
It's as though those scissors have snipped out
much of yesterday and half the last five minutes.
She's fifty-eight years old. Always meticulous,
she sets the books aside, trims an imperfect
edge. Neat curls of paper fall. I watch
the lessening. Her niece will love these books,
she smiles. And life is normal, so we say.

Jury Duty

I hate him. I'm not saying he's not a good
tennis player, I just hate him, he's a Mummy's boy.
This time of year I watch Wimbledon all night,

the only spell I get, when they're all asleep.
Don't hit it to him! Angles, angles! Kids
drive you crazy, I could happily kill the lot of them. Hey,

I got a letter, jury duty, came today.
And I'm up for it, Mum'll take the kids after school,
it's a break for me. That's called a net, you moron,

you're supposed to hit it over! She loves having 'em,
I'll never hear the end of it, mind you,
but I can't wait to get inside that jury room.

I was watching Henry Fonda the other night.
he's an actor after midnight, makes me bawl.
Love a good bawl, me, but if Frank hears, he comes out,

and gets romantic, so I keep it down.
Now hammer the idiot's backhand, it's his weakness!
If only they'd listen! Henry Fonda, yeah,

he turned that jury round. See on the news
that mother killed her three year old? How could she?
Double fault, good! I'd throw her in jail for fifty years.

So she did her block, she's a mother, I do my block,
it goes with the job, I could murder the little bastards,
but I don't, I watch the tennis! Out — it was out!

I don't believe this, he's used up all his challenges!
Where was I? Yes, she planned it, I hate the bitch!
My God, I should be a judge. Or an umpire.

Can't wait to be on that jury. Bloody hell.

Mad Bastard

A palette knife of pain the morning after
rouses. His ear is pierced, his heart. Breakfast
is booze. He allows that Jackson Pollack
might be his equal, but in a different style
so it's not relevant. He loves
the nothingness of working, the disappearance
of everything except the work. Except
the muse. The muse brings coffee.

She is his mirror and his DVD, she
turns life inside out, him inside out
he feeds upon her, fits her
like canvas onto frame, she fits him
like his mother, the first miracle. They
dance together, they make love, they spawn
this freakish, distorted, scandalous love-child
painting
sculpture
lithograph
for the world to turn its wealthy two-tone foot on, but
as the foot lifts
art that simply walks away, eternal as
love's impulse.

Drunk, he's laughing
obsessive, riven with unspoken oaths
showing her dressed and naked twenty times
flaunting, embalming her
so that she can live forever, dead.

Mastectomy

Afterwards, she undresses privately
or in the dark. And no-one gathered with her
at the earthquake statue in Skopje, Macedonia,
knows how it touches her. The railway station clock
opposite is frozen at five-sixteen,
the time the earthquake rolled like a locomotive
through the city. The statue shows a woman
lying in rubble, a breast torn off by debris –
Skopje ripped, deformed, betrayed by heaven.
Two other women chatter, she moves away.
This morning's Herald Tribune, she remembers,
said a science team from Denver University
has used a woman's own fat cells to partially
regrow a breast, as though that was enough.
The guide is signalling; they leave the statue
to see how Skopje has rebuilt itself

Early Morning Call

Six-thirty phone ringing like an ambulance.
Three years divorced, she's speaking up the line
Sorry it's early – I waited. I'm masked and wary:
our passion ambushed by the nine to five,
all roads led to the unregistry office.
Accident now, gravel, car flipped in ditch.
She was beside the driver. The death seat.
My mind draws breath.
Seat belts saved them, police car dropped her home,
she watched the sun rise, a red ball of life;
ringing to let me know, as I'll probably hear.
Suddenly as she talks, an unspoken island
of feeling, back before the morass.
Not reviving anything – too much water under those bridges –
but an epiphany: the passion, the wonder
those first days
quick and holy.
I'm politely sympathetic. We hang up.
The scorched earth hasn't been revegetated,
but the world has altered.
I'm a little more whole.

Stephanie's War

Standing on her balcony, she'd rant
down at our courtyard, *You're a nasty person,
you're very nasty*, though she scarcely knew you.
Stephanie was old and lived alone.

She had a screen of potplants by the railing;
she fed them, spoke to them and watered them
twice daily, which was chiefly when she opened up
on anyone caught walking in the courtyard.

She was convinced the people in the flat below
used radar to track her movements room to room.
She'd wake them, banging the floor at 2am.
A stream of haggard tenants came and went.

Stephanie was Jewish, she fled Warsaw
with her brother when the tanks came. She was twenty.
They went to Rome and lived as Gentiles, said
that they were married. Then Hitler followed her.

To earn a living, Stephanie was working
as a cook. Two SS officers moved in
nearby and offered her a job. Her brother feared
they might investigate if she refused.

For a year she made the Nazis' meals. Post-war
she wouldn't cook at all, ate only cold food,
and from her Burwood balcony she'd blast away
daily at the jackboot world besieging her.

Of course it had to happen, the tenantless
owners underneath called the authorities.
Two policemen in black uniforms, with a psych nurse,
knocked on her door. They said she had to pack

immediately and go with them. They took her
weeping to a police car, to a locked ward.
Her nephew got her flat, the potplants died
and Rome was Stephanie's eternal city.

A History of Touching

Arrival

Traffic's a tangle of lanes and lunges, patience and radio
programming. Bus ahead is loaded. A fool cuts in.
Brake hard. Bus stopping. Trapped, I miss the lights.

Around the corner, the world is suddenly different.
At the Writers Centre, cars come in like cows
for milking. I turn the key and power drops

like a towel. The evening's jacket now, not coat.
Figures unfold from cars. Stop, egret-stabbing
fingers through pockets, handbags – point and press,

locked. Life by remote control – it's left out here
in the car-park. Wildness is why we come here –
wildness, but not too crazy.

Assembly

For going to face the Minotaur, there are rituals. One actor spits
on the stage, another walks twice around the theatre. In the Writers
Centre we queue at the coffee machine, tying a thread of habit.
The script-writing class is bending an ant-trail to the giant-doored

TV room – smiles carried like men on stretchers, church-hush greetings
tip-toe. Some have private rituals – yoga and meditation.
TV writing is packed, you can earn a living (maybe). Advanced
Poetics is upstairs, the modernists hidden in Henry Lawson's Room.

As a woman nibbles her hair-ends, I wait in an alcove
doing homage to polystyrene and setting my head for a coven
of lyric lovers and velvet-eyed assassins. A square
glass table, shin-bang Japanese-low — I bruise my evening.

I'm watching the focused hunters trek forcefully through their lateness,
while the delicate isolates, maybe with most of the talent, scurry.
They understand that they need to work a room, but they'll
never do it, nor star at some series party. Still,

they know aloneness, farming the midnight self.
A late-coming girl in a trailing scarf and boots, a vision of style
and ambition, flits by. Briefly we smile as our eyes touch just for a moment
and I somehow suspect that I've kissed a crocodile.

Activity

We sit round a plastic topped kitchen table in the library
and skim spruced orphans across, our multiple A4 urchins
with tousled hair and shirt-tails needing more than a tuck.
Words can desecrate the sacred. We don't dare believe it.

There's no real reason psychopath hit-men shouldn't
be existential philosophers, talking Schopenhauer
and Nietzsche, but they can slow a poem down. As I say so,
I realise sinister energies lurk at our table.

Politeness wins. These are sensitive, beautiful people. What's next?
Indecent burial for a hurried snack of idea,
reheated fondue of thought in a tiny pot. Oh, dear.
I decide to say nothing. Next poem, though, is words that hang,

four o'clock in the morning words, insisting that there's a soul,
maybe not the immortal soul Father Ryan preached in pomp
and pulpit and Irish brogue all those Sundays ago – but an essence,
a solitary droplet of God. And whether or not that soul

is worth saving, it's surely worth knowing. This poem needs toughening
with dry bread, but it works, it's why we're here. The need
to touch. The sacred prays over us. Communion,
or the glimpse of it. Outside, it's dark now. In here, campfires burn.

We pull our rags together and go out.

Othello in Sydney

Love's a handkerchief at the blue water racing club, it flutters
as the bobbing plaything corks store up ambition among
the plankways, reputation riding the swell like a waterbed
as upstairs money hugs the sunshine. Marina water glints
its daggers below peaceful voracious seagulls
tacking and sliding in the slippery currents. North Africa
arrived and made a splash, photo in *Stay In Touch*, first night
at the opera, it's important. As Commodore, I welcomed him
and he knew his Sydney-to-Hobarts, his Fastnets and Bermudas,
a spinnaker from a single genoa. Black's a fashion
and women wept. He ran as I knew he would, stood, brand
"steadfast". But Commodore's tactical, I dropped two words, "jealous"
and "violent", people see what they want to hear, and it spreads
as the beds in these carbon-fibres are multifarious.
I tacked when I had to. They blackballed him in Double Bay,
he blamed his wife, she hadn't made the cut, but money's money,
you play your cards out East, and he thought that water views
were for the scenery. I'm not surprised to hear
he's being arrested, something about his wife.

Wagner and the NRA

The day after the break up time stands still
everything else is moving. Magnetic north's
now south. Absence becomes presence, and the house
has a different balance or tension. The telephone's icy
with silence. On the radio some clown
is dissing love and Wagner, and you're caught
in the slipstream like smashed roadkill, curious
to be alive and listening. The commentary
has you by the sleeve: someone is saying
Wagner was a meteor, and love-death
shook things up; he cites the clash between
Feuerbach telling Wagner life is crap
but love can save you, and Schopenhauer saying
life is crap and don't hold your breath for love.
What do they know? What do they really know?
The death of deep belief, he says, they're trying
to make sense of it.
You switch the station,
the NRA's saying guns are liberty
and life's a forest full of opportunities.
Distracted by anything – guns, air jockeys, murder
as your life disintegrates.
Wagner might have joined the NRA, he
understood bewilderment and blasting.
Everything in the kitchen's still the same mess
but the sense of what it means is breaking up.
At Station Wagner they're onto Gotterdammerung,
the world is ending, the gods have lost their power,
the universe is stranded. Then – applause,
the house is going crazy, stamping, clapping
like a thousand shotguns, they all love

annihilation when it's not their own.

You hit the Off, break out the booze. Inoculate.

You need to spend some time with Schopenhauer.

Balance of Power in a Theatre Foyer

Supergush hostess smile
welcoming box office chat
elaborate as kabuki
at the door of The Phoenix Playhouse
I wrote for years ago.
As she takes my ticket
I can't remember her name —
and she keeps saying mine
counting out my change
aware absolutely
she has me at her mercy.

Wolf Spider

Eight eyes an uncomfortable coven
in the 10 p.m. from Central, carriage of four,
including him, tattooed and sullen, cap
on backwards, and he stares at you, his eyes

disagreeing with his head that flounders, bounces
slightly as you rock through suburban badlands.
You focus on your newspaper, and then above
the edge you see him walking up the side wall

of the carriage towards you, freakishly eight-eyed,
eight-legged, hairy, crawling, stopping, giant fangs,
scuttling again towards you. A lurch, a stop,
the train is stationary and the shuffling

tattoo-parlour stumbles off three stops
before yours. The train readjusts its speed
around itself like skirts, you sway and settle
and its still there on your newspaper, the spider,

three rows of eyes, two huge for hunting, big
as searchlights, two more underneath, and then
a row of four adjacent to the poison fangs,
a cinema of eyes devouring you –

you try to brazen out the beast, you stare,
then turn the page, defeated... Your garden's dark
right to your door. They're watching, foliage eyes,
binocular, predatory. You turn the key,

let yourself in, turn on the light. You feel
you're safe. And yet that nasty watching's locked
in here with you, where your most likely killer
is reaching out, has just two eyes, and loves you.

The Diagnosis

I find her reading Timelines in The Herald,
the page that resurrects not just the dead
but marvellous lives. "This woman went through Belsen
then came out here and never hated anyone",
she says, "and I think that's heroic". An eye
for detail keeps her conversation lively
though Alzheimer's is hacking gaps; she checks
the clock and makes an educated guess
as though everything's normal: "I said coffee,
after this, didn't I". She fills the jug
and starts to set out cups, relaxed and practised.
I've watched her run a brilliant strategy
of cover, cope, delay – of managing
disintegration. But now this. Now cancer.
She pretends she's calm and steady
as she faces radiology and chemo.
At five this morning I crept out and watched
the sun begin its burn across the terrace,
and although we love and cherish her
dreadful questions walked the deck out there:
Do we lose her even if she stays alive?
Could there be mercy in that different loss?

Destinations

Dream Fellini

Diocletian's Palace here in Split
is a Fellini film set, ancient walls
with modern apartments roosted like new psychoses
in ruined heads. It's a three-hectare one-horse city
within pre-Christian walls, where the old Emperor
retired to die in an army camp of marble.
La Dolce Vita on the hoof is loose
among lunchtime's duelling blackboards and pizza ovens.
Above us, high-rise women are reeling in
their sheets and shirts on pulleys from *La Strada*
heedless of any lackey yelling *Cut.*
Life goes on down the road from the Temple of Jupiter.

Is the Wandering Jew non-Jewish? The idea
of no-home, of moving on, or being moved on
haunts Australia like a buried body. Voss
is better, there's a home but we're not there,
we're off exploring the world with camels and baggage,
ransacking the continents of want.
It's not a magpie thing, not a bringing-back
(though we bring back all the time, bring back all time) –
it's roots. It's desert plants. The frailty of things.

Everywhere the smell of sulphur. Why build here
on the hem of fiery rain? The Emperor
was a traveller who came home. You love the place
you're born. But he understood the violence
under us. With walls six metres thick,
this would endure, as he had, as we seek to.
A fortress, it has stood through Slavs and Avars,
twitch-fingered Croat kings, drunken Venetian
sailors and tax-crazed Turkish governors.
Il Duce came a Fascist re-imagined

Diocletian – the strutting circus strongman.
Death turned him upside down.

Time is a slow earthquake, conquest is
an adzing eye, a hunger for better chess
that turns a colony into a toll booth.
They're at it here, the land grab legions putting
the present to the sword, the Adriatic
captured and swarming backwards, shore transformed
as landfill lifts the homes of crabs. Modernity
is The Riva's modern hardscape shopping strip,
pilum straight lines of low-care palm trees popping up
like toothpicks, as glossy fashion conquers grandeur
and optimism ignores the smell of sulphur.

In an agnostic age, the certainty of a ruin
generates a Lourdes for unbelievers.
I head into the cellars, into dark,
like Voss into his cave. In these huge caverns,
the soul can nail down phrases of eternity,
but not full sentences. The Emperor touched
these walls that I can touch, but I can't touch him.
Yet Voss could travel mystically, and I
can hear the Emperor shouting. Life's about
distance, defeating it, resolving time
and separateness – the drop becomes a dram,
the egg is fertilised, the seed comes home.
Voss was lost and perished in the desert
but I can see a journey. I go up.

An Extra Day in Split

After fighting all the morning, we have lunch
through the Iron Gate, with medieval Venice
and ancient Rome all round us. Things are calmer
for Croatia and for us – the gift of war
goes on, though. I have gathered you'd prefer
to be in Venice for another day.
Pizzas and cappuccinos seem to help,
sitting at a table in the street
under three-storey clotheslines holding pants
by the ankles, shirts like slack-armed corpses.

Diocletian repaired the teetering empire
then, throat uncut, retired and bequeathed it
to maniacs and dutiful administrators.
But not to us, you say. Still, now it's ours,
I think. You read my mind. We both say nothing
as blue-jean shutterbugs flash the fierce old pagan's
mausoleum. His Christian victims made it
a cathedral, walking on his face to Mass.
You seem to share their feelings. *Can we get
out of here, these flashes give me migraine.*

Down in the gaping cellars, we're close to what
the Emperor saw. Like lives, they filled with garbage,
were left to rot. Then science dug them out.
Once archaeology is cleared away
history is hint and absence. I walk the centuries:
These caverns are the coffin but not the body,
I say. You say, *What did you expect?*
At the door's a turnstile, and we pay.

Evening thickens and the traffic fidgets,
I check the time, we head for the hotel.
At the cinema three streets away, Satyricon
has been revived, reviving ancient Rome
according to Fellini, cellulite
with a side of brothels. As we leave the theatre
real rain hammers us. We run and miss
our street and wander cursing in the dark —
Satyricon has turned into La Strada.
A taxi driver rescues us and robs us.
At the hotel, I trade rain for a shower
and as I stand there contemplating steam
the shower door slides open and you join me.
Fellini has a wonderful effect on you.

Invasions

Bleached tussock and bare rock up here in the mountains, not
a tree, not a thorn, just a road getting out of here
and nature crouching, showing her teeth to the kicking wind.
There must be sun sometimes but today there's only a knife
and it's just September. It looks like the crow-ticked mountains
above Cooma, but this is Croatia, the Krajina,
the nationalist wars of the Nineties began around here.
Men fought and died for this basalt scar tissue
this is ours, this is who we are.
Free settlers – I think of tough white men in New South Wales,
telling themselves, *We come in peace but the blacks want war*
while the blacks see only invaders. The wind wavers
and a raven hops into his contested sky.

The captive-animal city down through the trees is pinned
and small – I can understand why artillerymen love mountains,
eagle views and mathematics, it's king-of-the-world stuff,
mapped parabolas of wind and distance, and you don't
have to live in the bursting bodies, or see them as the granite
ocean reliquaries, as cobbles become shrapnel
and men and women die screaming as their bridges burn.
It must have been good up here and alive in the snow-scarf,
breathing the cold blowtorch morning. Poor bastards down there.
They'd shoot you for thinking that.

Massive ravines between somewhere and somewhere important,
the crop plains of the Po and the jagged commanding heights
of Slovenian peaks that not so much scrape the sky as cut its throat –
a country of grown-up romance, for Hemingway set
A farewell To Arms in these ravines – I read it in Sydney
in autumn, drinking coffee in Leichhardt, and the Soca Front
became horrible magic, not a land-grab by Italy in Nineteen-Fifteen.
Half a million died, soft city men like me. Now billboards

invite me to shoot the Soca rapids that today
aren't guidebook turquoise but factory-waste white as unseasonal rain
flushes down silt. And any dark shapes in the water are porpoise
canoeists flipped over, not fetid human lumber in puttees and greatcoats
rotting in an eddy or ditch.

In the language of winter, in the huddle of mental villages, massacre
and memory knot generations. *They raped us, tortured us,*
killed us for hundreds of years, we need to take back what's ours
and take revenge. The horror of human weather. Outside
the petrol station in the rain a raven skips. Some local Serbs
are arguing loudly that Muslims are Turks and should be in Turkey.
We detach and climb back into our bus and shut the door
but the voices of invasion are hot and angry and frightened.

The World's First Atheist State

3a.m. in Tirana, tenth floor of the Sheraton – yes, they have
      earthquakes here.
People need to believe and I believe
there won't be an earthquake. In the meantime, I'm wondering what
that old man thought in the middle of the night?
Catherine's asleep, out the window it's pitch, some firefly
streetlamps, some movement far off on what may be roads.
Did he have any shame? Doubt? Did he talk to the dead
buried in the rubble of his heart?
Here he was, Enver Hoxha, cooped up in World War Two
long after it finished, turning the nation into
a foxhole. Did he forget its partisans
drove out the German army unassisted?
No Russians, Americans or Brits.
Down in the lobby
the hotel's a tomb, the nakedness of an empty church,
a silent conversation of marble, glass, velvet –
you could be in Sydney, not Albania. My
jetlagged footsteps rave
about slave camps and pillboxes, seven hundred thousand rabbit holes
and citizens told they could pick off invading tanks
with small arms fire. The invasion never came,
the pillboxes stopped it, he said, this proved their value.
The lifts are vertical
high-speed pillboxes, efficient, shiny, not good in an earthquake.
      Coming down
I walked ten flights, going up I take the risk. The door-swipe
won't swipe first time, then the damned thing finally clicks.
      Catherine's still
sleeping. The pillboxes are small confessionals, a rough chatter of
      weeds
and spiders; haunted by lovers, they've taken half the nation's
teenage virtue. Make love not war. They're hated

by farmers, immovable reinforced concrete.
Excellent, though, in an earthquake.

Hoxha forbade cars. Now
in the apostasy
Mercedes rule the roads.
Stolen, says Blaz, our guide,
from all over Europe.
Blaz is Slovenian, from the neighbourhood.
They don't even change the plates.
They like driving round Tirana
with Swedish plates.
They get a kick out of it.
Albanians are different from their neighbours,
Croats are Catholics,
Macedonians are Orthodox,
but Albanians are Muslims –
families are clans,
they all answer to the father,
that's how they've taken over crime in Europe.

City guide Erik sighs,
Albanians are nominally Muslim,
there's no call to prayer,
most people have two children,
but what can you expect from a Slovene?

Morning is better. The earthquake has happened already,
these are aftershocks; the Party was smashed in elections
and people daily roll the dice. Over scrambled eggs
and strawberry jam at breakfast, we disinter Hoxha.
His atheist state had two Gods – Marx, whom he froze,
and Darwin, whom he ring-fenced with barbed wire borders.
He believed the best life is simple,
bicycles and bad roads –

bad roads slow down invading infantry. (They certainly slowed our bus,
six hours-plus for two hundred kays to Tirana).
But when do good intentions become murderous? *When*
a man becomes a prophet – pass the jam. This
morning's the city tour, we gather coats and cameras.
Albanians are watchful, diffident, they'll discuss
ancient ruins and modern gardens,
but to questions about the regime they're brief,
they glance around, or shrug, or change the subject.
Erik has priestly calm: *It's still too raw,*
it's bad luck, even. it's like discussing a war. And if you're older,
you're careful. Tricked out in new clothes
the regime hangs on.

In Tirana the sky blossoms, a crop of colours.
After Hoxha crab, the Mayor painted the city
as a high-rise Picasso gallery: lived-in snapdragons,
industrial Joseph coats, apartment slabs
in burly football stripes, offices with sea green arrows.
It leaps on your upward eye like Hallelujah!
There's a thirtytwo storey building limit, Blaz advises,
Because of the earthquakes.

Inhaling yeros
at a street stall,
sliced hot meat, onion, cucumber
in a bread wrap.
Ketchup?, she asks.
It isn't ketchup –
how can it be ketchup? –
this is Albania, not Brooklyn,
you can't read the writing.
Ketchup?, she demands.
She has a plan to feed
the eight-year-old filing bottles

in a crate in the corner
and the man playing cards at the table.
Ketchup, I abjure.

The Ottoman's rule was simple: pay our taxes
and we leave you alone; resist and we slaughter you.
Muslims paid lower taxes, so Albanians converted.
But Muslim Albania, occupied by Germans,
hid Jews and declined to hand over lists. Alone in occupied
Europe, it ended the war with more Jews than before it.
Then Hoxha, the new Prophet, rose up, and in the camps
among thirty thousand prisoners, Mohammed was a crime.

Distance sprints in daylight, the horizon
has fled from across the street. The lobby is a hive,
a praying congregation of strangers
in a bustling church
where God, the atheist, has died. It's a time
of leaving, a time of overseas remittances.
The hotel chains came in and a newer Jerusalem
festers. Catherine tries to exchange our dinars
for Croatian kuna as no adjoining country
will change Albanian currency.
Our bus cranks up for Dubrovnik. Off Skanderbeg Square,
from a discreet minaret the call to prayer.
The old drift in, and children. The ancient Illyrian highway
seeks out the coast
as the earthquake rolls prodigiously and slowly.

The Party Secretary at the Tower Of London

We took Circle to Tower Hill, and here we are
at Torture Central. Truth is, the human psyche
is well aware that fear will help you grab
what isn't yours, but whether you're a bikie
or a Brigadier, power's what you need to keep it.
William the Conqueror practised what he preached,
now its more subtle, velvet glove's the key:
Adolf was brilliant till he over-reached.

Yeoman Guards make show among the ravens.
They scream their spiel over a constant loop
of inbound jets. Tour ends in the chapel, Yeoman Guard
propped at the door for tips, forty in our group,
six tours a day, say, for five days a week,
they making a killing, Probably each other. Moving through
the Crown jewels, (just gold plated, incidentally),
was an army of French tourists – déjà vu.

Peter Sellers would have been beheaded here
for what he did with Princess Margaret.
Times change, but the tradition stays important
because it's national memory; and, bugger it,
it's money for jam, done right. This one's a classic.
The Tower's just a head-butt by the Queen
on the British public, yet they queue to get it:
most professional bit of spin I've ever seen.

William the Conqueror was called The Bastard.
It's a term goes with the job. Every MP thinks
they'd make a great PM, but that one's putty,
that one's a sex addict and that one drinks –
the baton in the rucksack usually
turns out to be a toothpick; all our lives
are simpler if I sort it out impartially.
The hardest ones are the ambitious wives.

This way's the old way – coals, the rack, the dungeon,
today it's civilised, with men like me
to guard your bank account and dampen down
the shit-faced barons and the bastardry.
I referee their wars and give the knuckle
to maniacs who'd murder you and your's;
behind the screen, anonymously, quietly,
I prop up you, the party, and the laws.

Helsinki Tan

The white bear's claws withdraw;
icy all-day night
held off with double doona and double vodka
eases
Helsinki swarms back from minus thirtysix
for a disciplined Nordic ravishing of summer.
A festival of breasts and pomegranates
fills the marketplace, sculptured Venuses
playfully selling to prickly libidos nothing but
selling hard
while there's still time.
                              The naked harbour sparkles
beside a dancing poodle and three trained cats
jumping for a widow's mite. In the parallel park
the iron-shelled statesman, frozen in the heat,
is captured by a pirate seagull, intent,
chip chasing, oblivious of tock
on tick. The holiday boys, two trumpets, French horn
and tuba tap wallets with Mozart and McCartney
hunting and gathering in the brief long days
before light tightens, tourists migrate
green park bleaches
before knife cold lays siege, sketching
that longer winter within.

Nagasaki Rain

Silence is always audible through the noise,
it's your watching soul
disturbed. The buzzing city is a laminate
pressed upon awful stillness. You arrive
among a Ninja whispering of rain
under a riot of tyres at
Victoria Inn, 6-24 Dougashou.

In this lobby they've buried the body of the desert
in art deco
plush English furniture complete with upright
Agatha Christie phone – you're in the Cotswolds
not Nagasaki
till in reception Japanese are bowing
as in the days of Queen Victoria,
when smuggled guns began this sad relationship
with high explosives.

In the lift's quietness you ascend like God, aware
of an itchy skin rash on your ankles. Hotel soaps?
Room 412, you splash on lotion, rub it in
hang your soaking socks over the towel-rack,
then step into the shoes
of invading armies back five hundred years
that burned across Japan's most Christian city.

Jesuit footfalls in the aisles
of this painted wooden church, modern veneer
on Armageddon. At Ground Zero you stand
before a high blackened chimney, potent as
a crucifix.

Peace Park down the road, a shuttle-shuffle place
with photographs in tiers of floors to terrorise
the human spirit into peace while, blocks away
devotees hover in pachinko parlours
firing exploding rounds like they're in Moscow,
New York, London – not in a nuclear graveyard.

What do you do when you're bombed back to the Stone Age?
You bury and rebuild, and learn to love
baseball. Now, in the silent lobby, waiting
for the bus, you're thinking it could be
yesterday, or Nineteen-Fortyfive, serene,
two minutes past eleven.

Japan-San

Kobe railway station
jackhammer paradise
granite scissors cutting
half the world to pieces
Years of ikebana
bring the Spring this morning
wild and placid as
Fuji-san's mystic twin
dipped in its mirror lake

Above Tokyo's centipede
footpaths swaying towers
dance like mountain maples
not a place to make love
when the earth moves. Stillness
on my thirtysecond
floor as cherry blossoms
burst in city parkland
orgasm of April

Faces in *shinkansen*
sitting still while hurtling
three hundred k's an hour
slow, inscrutable
The sword is sheathed in the heart
and centuries of ritual
wrap in bands of honour
volcanic human violence

Weather Gods

We're not used to this in Australia, we can do
this snowfield of cherry blossoms heaped upside down
upon blue sky, but not this rapture,
this unembarrassed crowd
sitting quietly on tarpaulins in a Tokyo park
meditating on eternity
in a single blossom. These upturned Shinto faces
understand the godliness of flowering, each petal
still an unwritten tombstone, locked into life
for moments, released by death, its easy letting go
its ultimate perfection.

Bone-fingering wind and slantwise rain
through the massed blossoms in Kanazawa's
Kenruko-en Garden as winter doubles back
and smashes April for the fun of it.
My sweater's in my suitcase, I know I'll catch my death.
I turn my back like a beast, and watch the bus
disgorge us like a rented grave. In a fusillade
of white tatters, we ambushed *gaijin* cluster
in the useless shelter of blast-porous cherry trees
as whichever God it is whips us. God-fearing Japanese
are all inside, except tough gardeners,
old women in red plastic, the weather's nuns,
gathering away the wrack that falls again behind them.
They know this is the cycle. In puckered ponds
the golden carp are happy enough, out of the wet
we force-march into, umbrellas bobbing black mushrooms,
each of us ferrying a plashing personal
downpour that soaks our shoes and trouser legs. Now suddenly,
salvation through the rainscape, the Museum
of Traditional Crafts, and shelter. We jump this ship
of nature to be warm and wet but dry.

On a switch of wind, the rain dwindles and dies.
We emerge like refugees, thanking Whoever,
a little glazed with ceramics, but revived. Indulgent sun
nails our shadows to the path and greases them
so they slide like happy trombones. A ragged crocodile
steps through the sacred foam of sacrificial
flowers, vestigial offerings. We have in mind
our own vestigial offerings of tibia
and fibula, so we tread carefully. The Japanese
see this wrack as the remains of generations
gone – the ancestors, the turning seasons.
Hard-working birds are turning their flight to fibres
for nests and breeding. Spring here is an industry.
In the pond, ceramic-smooth, the carp continue
their ancient tracery, and clouds lie on the water
as blossoms lay on the sky, each now the other.
This is where Gods come from.

The Economics of Bicycles

Fifteen per cent of journeys in Tokyo are pedal power.

Bicycles round up Tokyo's great rolling days
in circular perambularity
not on its limousine-wide arteries
but in its thigh-force market streets among
the neighbourhoods and kimonos. Yet driving
these journeys is a paradox: by law,
you must have off-street parking if you own
a car; to feed the mantis appetite
people with off-street parking rent it out
at Midas profits; Midas profits mean
you can afford a car - but you can't get one
without your off-street parking. So you cycle.
These profits drive a new ecology
in which consumerism, cash and greed
produce a world of thrift and exercise.

Space-Time Samurai

The samurai emerges from a wormhole
in 2012, escaping a war party
from 1870. He's in a ryokan,
an eight-tatami-mat room, with a rolled
futon on the shelf for laying out

by the girl while he's at dinner. Behind a door
he finds a porcelain room of shouting water.
He slides a paper window — in the street
are metal animals and ugly clothes,
not a kimono or yakuta in sight.

And yet this room's the same — the mats, the pictures
of Fuji-san, of cranes. He sees a cupboard
that's talking to itself. Feels it, it's warm.
He opens it, it's cold, and ninja light
leaps out. But no attack. The chilly cupboard

clinks, it's full of bottles and metal tubes
that feel like snow. On top, he finds a list
that's written in American, he's seen
the language of the ships that forced the ports,
shaming the Shogun and the ancient ways.

This cupboard seems the ruler of the room
and, like the foreign jangling street outside,
lacks grace. He's stranded in a nasty world.
As he unsheathes the consecrated steel
his honour understands what he must do.

Taj Mahal 1

Transit station. a camel market of coaches
disgorging pilgrims of love and architecture.
My ex-wife always wanted to come here,
a monument to undying love, she said.

The station is a mêlée – shouts, confusion,
centipedes of day trippers, couples holding hands.
If she was here alone she'd take a deep breath
and tolerate the crush. I have to stop this.

Armed soldiers with abrupt directional thumbs
and cocked trigger fingers check for guns and bombs
in the field of love. The search is brisk and thorough,
the atmosphere strangely calm, like a lawyer's office.

Red sandstone walls conceal the monument –
then, in a calculated square, quite suddenly,
four minarets, the dome and white façade –
love distilled. Abruptly, I can't breathe.

I want to stare at it, but stricken lovers
of photography have propped ahead of me
despite the crowd behind us pushing in –
love is a crush a pummelling, a smiling

riot. To escape, I veer down steps
to a quiet Muslim garden where, my camera
still in its case, I find myself in middle years
derailed in a memorial to loss.

Taj Mahal 2

You're walking inside the head
of a man who has lost his wife, and who honours her.
The white dome of his skull
is a tumult like a railway
station, people yelling, guides blowing
whistles that shriek like trains, the sound
reverberating from the walls and roof in a roar
that drowns the world.

There are ordinary things as well,
daily things:
inside this head, you're overcome by fear
for your wallet, the crowd is thick as a Mughal army,
thieves must regard this situation
as Shah Jahan regarded India.
Pigeons swoop like soft artillery
or puff and roost in delicate Persian lattices,
deaf to the pandemonium of grief.

Raised like an altar in the tomb's great centre
is a platform, two marble sarcophagi,
one for Shah Jahan, one for the beloved
dead suddenly in childbirth.

Despite all the noise of India, he's alone,
a crypt is his occupation.

People jostle, the crowd moves like tidal loss,
you're trapped in a circling clock
of empathy, romantic imagination
and grim pickpocket awareness.

Suddenly you're out on the sunstruck plinth
but still within his eyes –
a hungry hawk is driving down the sky
as pigeons and parrots scatter.
A pigeon is snatched from air.
In a world of captive crowds and mathematics
savagery has been restored.

Thick Black

White heresy — a cappuccino in Istanbul,
capital of Turkish, a contrary notion in the land
of spoon-standing, Sultan-harem-rallying, mouth-grab
short black, throat percolating slowly, mellowed with
white-powder finger-daubing spongy marzipan.
Everywhere that moustached headshake of disdain,
the headmaster look of Tourist or Infidel, not mild refugee
from chocolate froth swilling Sydney.
We found it in a narrow, flat, perpendicular-sided capillary
off Beyoglu's pedestrian mall, tram-strung and Melbourne-clanging,
beyond a hookah standing on the corner, past huddles of pensive
afternoon men bent over backgammon under ancient
sunblock of vine leaves —
an aluminium table and a married couple of chairs
opposite a mandolin-eyed music shop
with Billy Joel waltzing Piano Man through the Islamic
air. "Cappuccino?" The waitress nodded.
In the hissing of Constantinople, we'd come home.

Rhymes and Rhizomes

Impulse upon Rising

I shall wear this day like a garment,
I shall draw it upon my spirit reverently.
Abroad, I shall bear witness
to the bright dash of birds,
the diligence of spiders,
the patience of animals.
I shall absorb myself
in the visions of people
discovering the Indies in each other,
the music, the flogging,
the ropes of hold,
the flights of mind
the trudging in darkness.
I shall bear witness to blindness
and trumpet epiphany.
I shall affirm the muscularity
of love, and the relief of laughter.
And when night comes
I shall drop this day like a shroud
and disappear into the ether
in the hope of finding another.

Dawn Assembly

Sleep-struck, I'm standing in my careful kitchen
as sights and sounds come Hitchcocking, attacking
my rattled senses in a strange crowjacking.

A dawn-bred world advances like a jury
of blackshirt citizens who roost in trees
judging me by different gravities

as flightless, wombat-like and from a cave,
helpless and naked in a violent place
with murder competent to judge my case.

Trusting the Rhinoceros

Something this big wasn't meant to fly.
Fingers tight, breathing an act of control.
That thump means the wheels are up, but the world's wrong
with a rhinoceros in the sky.

Inert in a tunnel of hum and orange juice,
I've got National Geographic off the trolley;
open the page – tribes in the Masai Mara
know to leave the rhinoceros alone.

Grazing on clouds, devouring distances,
digesting time in the belly of a beast,
we charge at God. Science is a faith
that guards us like an angel.

Fasten seat belts. Trusting the rhinoceros,
I'm still dreadfully aware of the dropping window.
Through rigid fingers and controlled dentist-breathing
my heretic bones shout at my calm religion
that something this big wasn't meant to stop.

Defrocked Priest

This clockwork day he joins the congregation
gathered outside the lunchtime T.A.B.
He smokes and watches the open-sesame
doors wink at punters, touting quick salvation.
He knows the truth of hope, tamps out a careless
smoke on a post; then, thoughtful citizen,
he puts the butt into a small throat-lozenge tin
he carries for the purpose. This is holiness.
Beside the twitching doors, out of the sun,
are footloose angels with nowhere to go
holding religious newspapers marked in biro,
scuffing toes and waiting for their race to run.

At two minutes to two he presses Four,
ascends with Paul McCartney in the lift
along with Mother Mary. It was swift,
a bishop's summons showing him the door,
rage not that he'd lost his faith, but that he'd made
liaison with the Mayor's wife, *a known nutter*
who, whether it's men or horses, loves a flutter.
The search for this low-paid temp job's been a shit parade.
The lift doors open with a magic *ding*.
He puts his password (pony) in and glances round
at Alison; thank God that he has found
another who can only hope, and cling.

Let's Do Lunch

Time misquotes you, Alice didn't always
look like that, nor like my memory,
no doubt. And Betty – wry, shy, wiry Betty
with her swift incisions. We went to Sweden
together, saw the rocks and rectitude
and loved it in a northern, bracing way.
I care about these people as we order –
we break bread rolls and laugh, till Madge announces,
"I'm sixtyfive and I hate discussing politics"
to shut it down. My memory has failed me
on her frigid, rigid views. And so, politely
over hors d'oeuvres, we chat about the ferries
and views across those limpid Nordic lakes.
Some reunions can be large mistakes.

To a Mall Poster

Pre-teen nymphet naked of years,
beret, long hair, short skirt, selling
fashion to adolescent fears
from focus group researchers telling
all her secrets. The magic disappears

as soon as those Twittering other selves
own it, sending the mobile choir
chattering back to racks and shelves
in the departments of desire,
tweeting and buying eights through twelves.

Her eyes shine in a flawless face,
her ear-ring is a single pearl.
Moving about within the space
of all-grown-up while still a girl
she thinks the world's a happy place.

The lovely sexual youth she's wearing
sits in an innocent knowing stare
while her mother watches, bearing,
in a face touched by when and where,
the seeds of ancient disrepair.

A Larkin Love Story

Your cat rushed on the road, I couldn't stop
and killed him. I was just a rookie cop,
you were a nurse, and calm, and you forgave me.
We became lovers and, the next weekend, we
drove to buy a kitten, named him Chance
to mark our accidental road-romance.

Now I'm a sergeant, and you're a matron making
twice as much as I am, and you're breaking
my balls. Our poor old cat is now No Chance,
like me. I sit here watching you advance
along the footpath, carrying a load
of shopping. Then you step onto the road.

Kerry Packer, Olympian

I'm sorry but Kerry Packer doesn't
look like Kerry Packer in
these endless TV resurrections
as he hijacks cricket punching
holes in Bradman. We love power
even though he would have sacked us
we worship from a time-warp distance
his stallionness – this pious nun
he gave his cash to privately
called him an expletive ridden
saint, though others took a lesser
view, a lefty non-nun called him
a pole vaulter in the prick Olympics.
And whether he's with God or with
the other television greats
down in that other Green Room, truth is
watching his life reborn, the things
we love are the Olympian lies.

Sunday Conquest

A double bed is a kingdom of bounce and squirrel
energy on lazy Sunday mornings
for a tiny tyrant conceived here unimagined
who, equally demanding as the eye-glint,
burrows among bicep and breast to lie
in the overwhelming comfortable, comforting
smell of owned, known precious bodies.
In this faux democracy, (Doctor Spock and others
have much to answer for), the small, legged turbulence
flush with coltish morning wriggles, turns
till firmly ordered quiet.
Quiet persists for sixty seconds, then
back is braced on one flesh, feet on another flesh,
to prise apart the universe: such power!
Threats prevail, contentment comes, until
a sleepy sibling totters to the bedside
to be welcomed in with arguments of fairness
that fail with sibling's sibling.
If the usurper cannot be despatched
to hell if possible or to purgatory
at least, a pattern's set.
Freud knew this, and Goebbels, that loving father.
Killers come from happy homes as well.

New Privateer

In the derivatives melee
trucks take home bankers' take-home pay;
the party hit the street of Wall
as free for some went free-for-all.

Steal a Merc or catch a cab,
the latest smash was smash-and-grab;
but something's desperately askew
when the new black is black-and-blue.

It couldn't last, it wouldn't keep,
when Lehman landed in a heap
a desperate SOS was sent
for rescue – could the government

while staying out, please get involved
but only till the problem's solved.
It did. It worked. Too big to fail
keeps all the bankers out of jail.

Stop Watch

Silver body, cyclops in a glass,
lighthouse action swivelling a talking
beam;

stick fish dining on a reef of numbers,
guarding the perimeter of his base
each minute;

nervous tic, a twitching – edging forward
by little leaps, creeping towards murder
or a script kiss.

two hands struck off, abandoned bloodlessly,
single digit spinning in the air
razor alert;

tumbrel rolling, large wheel turning and
a swinging blade, time falling to a sudden
stop.

Unawares

Such a neat hand – it catches me unawares.
Pulling an old dictionary from the shelf
I open it, see the signature, and myself
back twenty years momentarily: intense
surprise, like pausing suddenly on stairs
to stop a fall. Strange undertones commence

that shouldn't, so I shut the cover. Yet
I've opened it a hundred times and missed
those measured loops while chasing down some list
of words. I check the book. The binding's frayed
spine bottom right, the random strands like jet
hair that might be gathered in a braid.

It's over. And to prove the magic's gone
I open up the page again: mere flat
ink on paper. Furious loving at
any provocation. Certain things withstand
adjustment. I close the cover, holding on
to older darkness, weigh it in my hand.

Brotherly Love

I'm contemplative, shy with women, serious —
he's visceral, impulsive, brotherly
only in blood. *He's certainly not otherly
inclined*, one woman giggled, *He's a riot.*
I talk too much, where he's imperious
and kisses them on the mouth — and women buy it.

He loves John Lennon, sings his heart, obsesses;
Jane plays piano and hoards minutiae
such as, *What year did Buddy Holly die?*
She belts out Joplin (Scott, not Janis). Sweet
talk explodes to fury. Then he confesses
he's wrong, quite often lying. And they eat.

She's put on weight. They're like my tank of fish
with their circling and returning and their prowling.
One evening she's laughing, then she's howling.
I wrangle sodden handkerchiefs, and see
her passion and her pain. Ignored, I wish
sincerity could out-trump vanity.

Michael the Vicar

He can hear her in the pipes' ungodly bang
as the tap slaps off,
shoved with her wrist – she lets her fingers hang
rather than grip. She's closed the door, it's black
here in the bedroom. Bang! He sees the pain
in her absent face.
She won't be here in bed again
for half an hour. He'd comfort her, poor pet,
but she's told him, don't come out, she gets upset.

If he asks her in the morning she'll just say
There's nothing, and there isn't.
The doctor says, *Wear and tear, and by the way,*
you need to give up smoking, which she knows.
His constant lectures mean she only goes
there when she must.
She's coughing. Michael tracks the sounds
and tries a prayer, knowing at 4a.m.
pain is God's plan for them.

4711

You dabbed it on like goodness, and the scent
intoxicated me. Once, to impress,
I looked it up, found a Cologne address
during Napoleon's wars. You didn't care –
history was now, and now must be mis-spent
with pheromones like music in the air.

But pheromones confuse. I'm readdressing
your letters in the kitchen, and your favourite
scarf's in my pocket. Though I'm over it
I can inhale and in an instant go there.
Insane. For there I was, and you confessing
you'd followed other pheromones elsewhere.

Dear God, it's March

Yesterday was Christmas (wet again),
today it's March, next Friday it's July.
I'm caught in a time warp — Einstein's metronome
of individual time for everyone
ticks away the universe, and me.

A school week used to take six months mid-term,
bad weather, shitty teachers and exams.
The first two weeks of Christmas holidays
took more or less a fortnight, sleeping late,
hanging at the mall on Thursday nights,
watching Security watching us, the cops
trying to look like heroes, specially
the chicks. The next two weeks took up a year —
nothing on TV, some girl you liked
said, *See you Saturday*, which took forever.

Later on, six months took a week — the mortgage,
promotion, flat chat at work, the kids, school meetings,
*You were there? Well, we were going, last minute,
you know how it is. The same for you, I know,
you're just a better planner, good you made it.*
Butter wouldn't melt, she's such a bitch.

You know when you retire there'll be time.
Then the house is falling apart, tomorrow's book club
to keep the mind whatevering, the grandkids
need babysitting while they're both at work
to pay the mortgage, then there's doctors. *Don't be
a stranger, can it be a year?, Two? No,
it can't be, I had no idea.* I never
seem to draw breath, but I'm getting further behind.

I used to wonder why Elizabethan
noblemen and other idiots
risked the axe in some mad grab for power
when the odds were piled against them.
Now I understand. You've only got a blink,
you might as well die trying.

Yes, Spring

The trees are green, the stretching air is gravid
with hay fever and hope. The parliament
of sun is newly sat and rowdy, avid
for opening. In the park, the scent
begins of coloured riot. Tumescent shoots
arise from flower beds, as the iron law
dictates that days of hectic hot pursuits
end in long evenings of *je t'adore*.

Spring nights quicken. The fight from a disgorging pub
is full of the strewn exuberance of youth
with yeasty, bubbling hormones by the tub.
Down little lanes the happy naked truth
is tested against fences. In the better bars
the spirits are high octane, and the looks
from lady law practitioners to rising czars
of finance are enough to burn their books.

In shopping centres, Spring is licensed lust
for one more round, a final quick cartoon
permitting merry flaunting of the bust
as busy sextants measure afternoon.
The registers are ringing in the stores
and optimism spreads like an aroma
while on the unwrapped beaches, naked pores
begin to sing the song of melanoma.

Acknowledgements

Poems in this book have appeared in these newspapers and magazines:

Sydney Morning Herald, The Australian, Canberra Times, Quadrant, Cordite, Medical Journal of Australia, Eureka Street, Five Bells, Famous Reporter, Blue Dog, Social Alternatives, Blue Giraffe, foame, The Mozzie, poam (Melbourne Poets Union); and in the anthologies *The Attitude of Cups* (MPU), Poems 2013 (Australian Poetry) and *The Stars Like Sand – Australian Speculative Poetry 2014*.

Special thanks for their workshopping skills to the Walter Street Poets at Hurstville and Wednesday Night Poets at the Writers Centre at Rozelle, and to John Carey and Norm Neill for their comments on many of the poems.